the gift of prayer

TEACHING CHILDREN TO PRAY

SUSAN IRWIN

Wipf & Stock
An Imprint of Wipf and Stock Publishers
199 W. 8th Ave., Suite 3
Eugene, OR 97401

www.wipfandstock.com

PAPERBACK ISBN: 978-1-6667-3413-3
HARDCOVER ISBN: 978-1-6667-2966-5
EBOOK ISBN: 978-1-6667-2967-2

TO MY FAMILY

My parents and parents-in-law who loved us enough to teach us to pray;

my husband Graeme, a constant inspiration to me of faithful prayer;

my children, Josh, Sam, Caleb and Phoebe, with whom I have had the
joy of growing together in prayer, and Eva, my beautiful daughter-in-law;

and Silas and Leon who now join the journey of blessing the next generation.

TO MY TEAM

I am so grateful to Rosie for the hours of editing she has done to enable this to happen.

I am blessed every time I see another of Jen's beautiful illustrations inspired by her own boys.

I am thankful to Mylan and her ability to design in a way I could never do.

You make a great team.

SUSAN IRWIN AUTHOR

JEN LAMB ILLUSTRATOR

ROSIE GOMAN EDITOR

MYLAN CHEN-OUGH DESIGNER

INTRODUCTION

OUR FATHER
WHO ARE YOU, GOD?

IN HEAVEN
WHERE ARE YOU?

HOLY BE YOUR NAME
WHAT ARE YOU LIKE?

YOUR KINGDOM COME, YOUR WILL BE DONE,
HERE ON EARTH AS IT IS IN HEAVEN
WHAT DO YOU LOVE?

GIVE US THIS DAY OUR DAILY BREAD
I NEED HELP.

FORGIVE US OUR SINS
I WANT TO BE ME.

AS WE FORGIVE THOSE WHO SIN AGAINST US
I WANT TO BE LIKE YOU.

LEAD US NOT INTO TEMPTATION BUT
DELIVER US FROM EVIL
I WANT TO FLOURISH.

FOR YOURS IS THE KINGDOM, THE POWER,
AND THE GLORY, NOW AND FOREVER
I WANT EVERYONE TO SEE HOW
WONDERFUL YOU ARE.

One of the most wonderful roles as a parent is as a teacher and mentor to our children as they learn to pray. As we do this, we are honoring the beauty and uniqueness of our children, who long for a deep and lasting relationship with their creator — the heavenly Father who loves them and knows them even more intimately than you do as their parent.

You will not always be with them as they grow and mature, but their heavenly Father is always with them. How blessed is the child whose parents have led them into this relationship! They are never alone, they always have a vision for their future, and on a daily basis they hear the voice of the Spirit leading them to become the people they were created to be.

When we teach children to pray, we often focus on teaching them to ask. Asking is an essential part of prayer but prayer is so much more than this. It is about a two-way relationship, an identity and a calling. Children need to experience this relationship, to know their identity, and to live in their calling in order to be fully functioning adults. When Jesus taught his disciples to pray, in what we know as the Lord's Prayer, he taught them much more than to come with a list of requests. I believe that Jesus' teachings on prayer will bring children to a new place in their understanding of God. They will discover who God created them to be, and the purpose and calling in their life. They will learn how to be calm in the middle of stress, find hope, bring blessing to others, and engage with the love of God.

Prayer is not something we do as a formula — it springs from relationship.

So, even though in our home we have always made it a habit to pray together and read the Bible together daily, we don't restrict it to set times. Prayer can happen as we are driving, walking, eating, or simply going about life. "Let's pray for that person we see having a hard day." "Let's thank God for this wonderful day together!" "Let's forgive that person who upset us." "Please show us what to do!"

As you pray with your children regularly, consider the Lord's Prayer. It reflects Jesus' relationship with God the Father, and Jesus encourages us to pray in that same way — to have that same relationship. By exploring the way Jesus prays, with your child, you will be helping to develop their understanding of God and life in all its fullness.

our
father

Who are you, God?

When children are learning to pray, they need to know who they're praying to. Who is God, and who is he to them? Answering questions like these can help them start to understand the relationship they have with God, and why they want to pray:

What is God like?
What does he think of them?
How should they approach him?
When can they approach him?

How do you think of God when you come to him in prayer? The way you address him and talk with him will affect how your children see him.

When Jesus prayed, he always addressed God as "Father." As a parent you also need this revelation of God; he *is* your Father, and knowing him in this way changes everything.

Children to need to know that God is a wonderful Father who is always thinking of them and always cares for them. They need to know this now so that when they are not with their families, they know they still have a Father to call on who is always with them. When Jesus taught us to pray, he reminded us firstly that we are in the presence of our Father and that when we pray, "*our* Father," we are also a family under him.

As our perfect heavenly Father, God offers us security in our identity as his child, hope for the future, and comfort in his presence. It can be tempting to want to offer all of these things to your children yourself, and although God truly uses you to give your children an understanding of what it is to be secure hopeful and comforted, we are only human, and we can't do t perfectly the way that he can. God is always there: at home or at school, when they wake and when they sleep, when they're with you or when you're somewhere else. He sees to the very depths of their longing or insecurity, beyond what you know and what they're able to express, and he is there with them even to the bottom of those depths.

For I am the Lord your God who takes hold of your right hand and says to you, Do not fear; I will help you.

ISAIAH 41:13 NIV

When I was about five or six years old, I was lying in my bed praying one evening when I felt a most wonderful sense of the presence and the love of God. From the bottom of my heart I expressed to the Lord how much I loved him. At that moment I had a profound experience of the love of God. It was like being flooded with life and love. When I woke up the next morning the sense of his love was still there. I had the sense that everywhere I went God was holding my hand — my right hand, which he promises to take hold of in Isaiah 41. The memory is so clear I can still feel it. I hadn't read that verse from Isaiah 41, but I experienced it. The Holy Spirit was very present with me speaking his truth into my life, even as a child. He was pursuing me with his love and I didn't know it until I encountered him.

God is present with you and your child. He will speak to your children by his Spirit because he loves them. You may have given birth to them but he created their inmost being and knit them together in your (or their mother's) womb (Psalm 139:13).

You can trust him to do more for your child than you can imagine.

Never limit your child's ability to experience the love of the Father firsthand. As you teach your children how to pray, expect them to have revelations of the love of God and to experience his presence.

FOR KIDS

With your parent, carefully fill a container with some sand, rice or small seeds. Try together to count the grains (you don't have to finish counting them all if there are too many, but give it a try!) How many are there – Fifty? Three hundred? More than you can count?

Every single moment you are thinking of me!
How precious and wonderful to consider
that you cherish me constantly in your every thought!
O God, your desires toward me are more
than the grains of sand on every shore!
When I awake each morning, you're still with me.

PSALM 139:17-18, TPT

God's thoughts about you are more than the number of grains of sand on the seashore! There were so many grains in the container you just counted, and it was such a small container. Think about how much sand there is at the beach — God's thoughts about you are more than even that! It's so wonderful that he loves us and cares for us more than we can imagine!

Your parents think about you a lot, as they take care of you through the day, and God is just the same.

He helps take care of you because he is your heavenly Father. Even though you can't see him, he is still there to give you the love and comfort that you need.

You can talk with him at any time, telling him the things you're excited about, or what has made you feel upset. You can tell him when you're scared, or feel lonely or mad, and he will always listen and always love you.

FOR PARENTS

Ask your children: what would they like to say to their heavenly Father today? Is there anything you would also like to ask him?

Sharing some of your prayer points with your children is a great way of helping them to understand the great range of what they can ask for, and of knowing that God is meeting your needs as well as their own.

Encourage your children to say their prayer needs out loud, or in their heart — both ways are prayer.

Now that you've prayed, ask your children to take some time to listen to what God might be saying back. Explain that they probably won't hear words out loud, but they might "hear" an answer in their heart or mind. Parents, you listen, too! Share with each other what you felt or heard.

Read Psalm 139:17–18 again and pray together tonight as you go to bed. Remember that your heavenly Father is there with you, loving you and watching over you all through the night!

in
heaven

Where are you, God?

In order to lead your children well, you need to lead yourself well. This simply means allowing God to reveal to you what's happening in your heart and mind, and then following his lead.

There's a beautiful prayer found at the end of Psalm 139 that you can pray as a parent who longs to do this journey of parenting well. I encourage you to pray it regularly, and allow the Father to transform you. Over time, his influence in your heart will give you a much better understanding of how to lead your children with wisdom and kindness. A person who is not open to the Father's searching gaze tends to lead more from their own limited strength and knowledge, but by opening ourselves to him, we parent instead as a person who is acquainted with his wisdom and grace.

God, I invite your searching gaze into my heart.
Examine me through and through;
find out everything that may be hidden within me.
Put me to the test and sift through all my anxious cares.
See if there is any path of pain I'm walking on,
and lead me back to your glorious, everlasting ways—
the path that brings me back to you.

PSALM 139:23-24 TPT

So, what does all this have to do with the line from the Lord's Prayer, "In Heaven?" Begin by asking yourself how you see Heaven. Where is it in relation to you? What is it about Heaven that makes it significant to pray, "Our Father in Heaven?"

Heaven is not as far away as many think. Our Father is in Heaven, but Heaven is very near, and children need to know that closeness — as do you. Imagining Heaven as a million miles away just because we can't see it, is not helpful and it isn't true. Heaven is close. That true image of God and his kingdom close by is an important reminder to children that he hasn't left them alone. We are assured in the scriptures that his presence is with us always. You could teach them this verse in a version of your choice:

> Truly, blessing and mercy will be with me all the days of my life; And I will have a place in the house of the Lord all my days.
>
> PSALM 23:6 BBE

When we see Heaven as far away, it is easy to let this world fill our thoughts and conversation with the bad things that are happening around us, engendering and perpetuating fear in the world and in us. Instead, let Heaven fill your thoughts! As it says in The Passion Translation,

> *Yes, feast on all the treasures of the heavenly realm and fill your thoughts with heavenly realities, and not with the distractions of the natural realm.*
>
> COLOSSIANS 3:2 TPT

How much of your conversation is taken up by complaining about people or situations in our lives and in the world? Your children overhear what you say, and it is influencing their thoughts. Be intentional with what you are bringing to their minds. Speak about good things around your children — let them feel secure and give them a strong basis for bringing good into the world as they grow.

Keep your thoughts continually fixed on all that is authentic and real, honorable and admirable, beautiful and respectful, pure and holy, merciful and kind. And fasten your thoughts on every glorious work of God, praising him always.

PHILIPPIANS 4:8 TPT

By speaking about good things, we help our children to dwell on God and his solutions instead of focusing on the problems. We remind them that Heaven is near, and so is their loving Father.

Every good and beautiful thing in the world is a taste of Heaven.

We rejoice that we can know these things and one day experience them fully. So when we pray, "Our Father in Heaven," we remind our children that we have a Father who lives in the realm of great power and goodness. He creates everything that is beautiful and he is very close to us.

His nature is love and he will follow us with his kindness and mercy every day for the rest of our lives.

I'm sure that there are lots of things you love in this world: people who you enjoy spending time with, places that make you feel safe or excited, ideas that really make you think, beautiful parts of nature where you can explore, and stories that inspire you!

All of these things came from God, and can show you a tiny bit of what Heaven is like.

Heaven is God's kingdom — a place full of good things, and full of God himself — and it is so close to us that we can see parts of what Heaven is like, even here on Earth. We can see Heaven in the beauty and intricacy of nature. We can feel it when we hope for something good. We can experience it in the loving relationships we have with people. All of these things are from Heaven, and all of them are because of God.

Think about some of the people, places, ideas, parts of nature or stories that you love and thank God for them! Thank him that Heaven is so close that we get to experience part of it now. Thank him that he is so close that his good things can be in Heaven *and* on Earth. He really never leaves us alone.

As you lead your children in prayer, invite them to either say their own prayer or use a prayer like this one, both of you adding your own personal touch as you go with the names of people, places, and individual joys and experiences:

Our Father in Heaven, thank you for this day!

(What things happened today that you loved? Say them here!)

Thank you for the birds and the animals, the flowers and the trees, the lakes and the streams, and the sun that rises and sets over them each day.

(What do you love in creation?)

Thank you for creating everything we see! Thank you for the life we live, and for making each person different.

(Which people are you thankful for today?)

Thank you for Jesus, who died for us so that we can live a wonderful life here on earth, and one day go to heaven just for believing in him. What an amazing God you are!

In Jesus' name, Amen.

holy be
your name

What are you like, God?

Sometimes we pray words because they're familiar to us or we're told to use them, but we don't really know what they mean. This is natural for children, but many grown-ups are still praying things we learnt long ago without considering why.

"Holy be your name" can easily fall into that category. We often pray this as a statement, which it isn't. It doesn't say "Holy *is* Your name". Instead it's presented as a request: "Holy be your name" – or in other words, "Please, may your name be made holy." Why would Jesus have us ask for God's name to be holy? Isn't it holy already? It is — but as we ask him for this, we are asking for a change to be wrought in ourselves.

When we speak of the name of God, we are referring to his authority, his character and his very being.

Praying for his name to be holy, is asking that in our hearts, in our words, and in our actions we would represent the holiness of God. We ask that he would be honored in everything we do, say, and think. We ask that we would do nothing that would make people think less of him. " Holy be your name" is about humbling us, and our heart's attitude towards our heavenly Father. We recognize his absolute authority and power, his character of grace and kindness, and his very being of joy and love.

Prayer is a two-way relationship. You are teaching your children to develop a relationship with God of love and honor, where he loves and honors us and we love and honor him in return.

We tell him what we love about him. We tell him that we love him. We love God by loving the people around us, because he loves them too. We also love Him by obeying His word. The reason we pray, "Holy be your name" before we ask for anything, is because it reminds us that even though God is our kind and generous Father, his very nature demands our honor and reverence. We must avoid treating him like a servant or genie, just there to give us what we want when we want it.

As a parent, teaching your children to pray begins with the way you talk during the day. Your children need to hear you modelling this holiness and reverence, which can also be done in your relationship with them. Tell your children what you love about them. Tell your children that you love them. And then be intentional in telling your children what you love about the other people in their word – your family, extended family, and people of significance in their lives such as teachers and friends. Parents who are modelling honor teach their children to see those around them as worthy of honor and respect because they are created by God, made in his image and loved by Him. You can model honor even when you discipline your child, by separating their actions from their identity, and by refraining from demeaning them. Even when they have done something that needs to be corrected, they are still God's beautiful creation. This is what our heavenly Father also does for us.

I heard a story about a family who had guests over for dinner that goes like this:

As they sat down at the table the dad asked his six-year-old daughter to pray. She replied, "I wouldn't know what to say."

Her mother said, "You can do it. Just say what Mummy says."

The little girl closed her eyes and said, "Dear Lord, why on earth did I invite all these people to dinner?"

Children hear more than we realize and we model more than we realize. As you lead your children into a relationship of honoring God with their lips and with their lives, you are teaching respect for God and people.

In a culture sorely lacking in honor, followers of Jesus can be countercultural simply by intentionally living as people who honor and respect others.

God is your heavenly Father who you can always trust in everything.

This is because he is holy. Holy is a bit of a strange word so let's have a go at understanding what it means.

You can describe most things by saying what they are like. For example, blue, red, and green are all colors. Dogs, lions and horses are all animals. All these things fit into groups or categories which are like each other. But God can't fit into any group or category. He is bigger, and greater, and more powerful, and more loving than anyone. He is the most intelligent, the most creative, the most fun and the most powerful person in the universe.

Another thing that makes God holy is that he is perfect. There is no bad in him at all. He never has a bad thought, says a bad thing, or does a bad deed.

Everything he does and everything he says is good and perfect, and true.

When you look at the stars at night, you can think about how great God is and you can thank him in your heart. When you think of how good he is and how he loved you enough to send Jesus to rescue you by giving his life for you to bring you into God's care, you can thank him in your heart.

This is what we call worship. We think of how amazing God is and we thank him in our hearts or with words that come from our hearts.

God lives in you by his Holy Spirit and he wants to make you holy so that every day you become more like him. He has a big plan for you.

Even though holiness is difficult to describe to children, an understanding of the holiness of God develops in children the ability to trust him. They see how wonderful he is, and they know that there is no one greater than him to rely on.

An understanding of holiness is the beginning of worship.

Ask your children to share what they love about God being perfectly good, all-powerful, and all-loving.

Then sit and imagine that this amazing God is present in the room right now. Take some time to do this in silence. How does that make you feel? This is the start of worship.

God gave us his Spirit so that we could become more like he is.

Share with each other how you would like to be more like him and pray for one another. Pray that people would see that you are like Jesus.

your kingdom come, your will be done, here on earth as it is in heaven

What do you love?

Fairy tales are often based on the idea of kingdoms.

The adventures, battles, victories, and resolutions resonate deep within us.

We love the stories where the wicked ruler is overthrown so the good king or queen can take their place. When evil is defeated and goodness reigns — when peace and harmony fill a land — it is because a kingdom is led by someone who loves and cares for its people. In a kingdom where goodness reigns, there is joy.

In our hearts, regardless of our age, we long for that sort of kingdom. We look for it in the world we live in, desiring good in the leaders of our country, and voting with the hope of finding someone who will lead us towards such a life.

Parents can encourage their children to hope for this kingdom by exposing them to examples of it. One way is to read good books together. There are many classic stories where good conquers evil, which resonate within our spirits because we know we were designed for something more. The earthly longings reflect our desire for the perfect kingdom. Gladys Hunt, author of "Honey for a Child's Heart," says, "Reading should offer the solace of hope and goodness, of another world where truth and right triumph."[1]

1 Hunt, Gladys. Honey for a Child's Heart: The Imaginative Use of Books in Family Life, Fourth Edition. Grand Rapids: Zondervan, 2002.

As a parent you can find great books and stories that will help you build this hope and raise your children to fight for the great kingdom of grace where Jesus is the king. Your reading time helps build a worldview which helps with prayer.

If you teach your children intentionally, and bring stories of goodness and truth into their world, when it comes to praying, "Your kingdom come," they will have a deep understanding of what a good kingdom is like.

They will know they are praying, along with you, for God the Father to be the king who brings goodness and peace. They will long to pray for a world where evil is destroyed (rather than people), and people live lives of joy and abundance. Their prayers will go beyond their own needs as they are raised to take responsibility to pray for the world.

One thing we don't always learn as children, and therefore don't understand as adults, is that this kingdom begins in individual hearts and minds, beginning with yours. When you pray, "Your kingdom come," you are asking for the faith, the hope, and the love of God's kingdom to be ever present in your heart. It's difficult to ask your children to believe that you desire his kingdom of goodness if you don't walk humbly with the Lord yourself. Take some time each morning to pray for the Kingdom of God to be visible in your relationships with others and that you would be a model of someone living in the Kingdom of God.

Your children need to see God's rule and reign in your life at home when the doors are closed and no-one else is watching.

When my children were little, I made the decision that I would only speak to them in a way that I would be happy speaking if someone I didn't know well walked into the room. I wanted them to trust that I was the same person in private and in public, so that I could be a better representative of God's kingdom in their lives. I can't say I always achieved this, but I set this goal before me, and recognized when I failed, then did my best to fix it.

As you teach your children to pray, "Your kingdom come," help them give their fears and worries to the Father who cares for them.

In his kingdom, he takes over our fears and asks us to let him handle those situations. Jesus said,

"Are not five sparrows sold for two pennies? Yet not one of them is forgotten by God. Indeed, the very hairs of your head are all numbered. Don't be afraid; you are worth more than many sparrows."

LUKE 12:6-7 NIV

Remind your children of their value to God, and let them know they can give their fears and worries to him.

As you teach your children to pray, spend time simply talking to them. Ask them about their day — the happy things and the sad things. Remind them that in God's kingdom, he can use it all for good. Let them know that as we bring the sad things to our Father, he can return joy to our hearts because he is the King who handles these things. These conversations will develop your relationship with your child as well as with God.

As you take time to listen, to talk, and to laugh together, you model what prayer is really like — not a shopping list, but a living relationship with the most kind and wonderful God who enjoys our company.

Finally, as we pray, "Your kingdom come," children need to know that they are princes and princesses in the Kingdom of God.

God is King over it all, and since he is their heavenly Father, that makes them not just his subjects, but a prince or princess.

In their high position they get to experience all the goodness of God's kingdom, and they also carry the joyful responsibility of helping their Father to care for his kingdom and to reveal it to others. When they are kind and loving, when they are merciful and forgiving, they help spread the Kingdom of Goodness and conquer the evil in the world.

Imagine being the leader of a country or kingdom. You would be in charge of so many things, while you tried to take care of all of your subjects.

You'd need to make sure sick people were able to get help, that there were places for people to go and learn, that roads were smooth and easy to travel on, that there were parks and playgrounds for kids to use, that there was enough food to feed everyone in your country, that the laws were fair and safe for everyone — and probably lots of other things too!

Can you think of anything else important in taking care of a LOT of people? That is all a lot of responsibility, and it would be very important for the person in charge to want to care properly for the people in their kingdom. If they didn't care, or weren't trying, then a lot of things would fall apart. Bad leaders can really hurt the people they have power over when they're not doing a very good job of leading. But good leaders can make sure that their people are protected, and safe, and happy. God is an excellent leader. His kingdom, Heaven, takes the things that are wrong, and turns them right.

His kingdom is built on love, and when he loves us and gives us power to love others too, then all of the kingdom works together for good!

As people who love God, we are from his kingdom, and we get the goodness of his leadership, even while we live here on Earth.

In fact, God has made it our mission to help him bring the goodness of Heaven to Earth, so we get to spread his love here, and help make Earth a better place.

What did you experience from God's kingdom today? What made you happy? Talk about it with your parent, and thank God for those good things!

What else happened today? Was there something that made you sad or worried?

You are so precious to God — the sad or scary things that you experience here, he can work into something good. You can tell him about your fears and worries, and know that he is the King over them and he can take care of you. Jesus said,

"Are not five sparrows sold for two pennies? Yet not one of them is forgotten by God. Indeed, the very hairs of your head are all numbered. Don't be afraid; you are worth more than many sparrows."

LUKE 12:6-7 NIV

That means that God cares for the little things, the big things, and you — and because he is your heavenly Father, he is with you even when you're worried.

Since God, the King, is your heavenly Father, that makes you a prince or princess in his kingdom!

You get to help him bring his kingdom here.

Ask God what good things you can do to help spread his wonderful kingdom, and listen!

FOR PARENTS

Parents, more than anyone else in the world, see the good in their children. You see their gifts and talents. You are excited about their potential.

Those feelings of delight in your child come from the heart of the Father. As his representative in their lives, you have the power to speak strength and encouragement into them.

Tell them what you see about them that makes their role valuable as a prince or princess in the Kingdom of God. You will notice personality traits, skills, and beautiful qualities of character. You may also notice some things that annoy you or concern you. There is a flip-side to all of these.

Ask God to show you the flip-side, and speak it out. For instance, a strong-willed child has the potential to become the person who does what right even if everyone else is doing the wrong thing. Their strong will is a strength. A shy child is often a deeply sensitive child who has an innate ability to sense what is going on in others which enable them to be a blessing and encouragement to people. Their shyness will be manageable as they grow in him and can become a strength.

As you pray for your child, thank God for creating them with all these wonderful qualities which he will use to bring his Kingdom into the world through his princes and princesses.

Here's a little prayer you could all learn off by heart.

Often as children lie in bed at night, having a prayer to pray and meditate on, leads to a deeper experience of God's presence.

Hi, it's me, just come to pray
And thank you for a fun-filled day!
You've been with me, so I know you've seen
All the great exciting things.
But also when I'm sad or cross
I know you love me, no matter what!
So help me rest and go to sleep
And feel the peace of your love for me.

AUTHOR UNKNOWN

give us this day our daily bread

I need help.

You may remember learning this part of the Lord's Prayer as a child, and wondering why you were praying for bread when most days it was readily available. Your children most probably wonder the same thing.

At the time Jesus first prayed this prayer, bread was a staple of the diet of the Jewish people, and was also known as a powerful symbol of God's provision. If you read the story of the Israelites in the wilderness, in Exodus 16, you'll see that when they were hungry they cried out to God, and he provided them with manna (a type of bread) that rained from Heaven. They receive an abundance, but it only lasted for that day, and they had to rely on him again for provision the following day.

When Jesus invites us to pray for our daily bread, He reminds us that we need God's provision for our lives each day. This request tells us to expect good — to trust each and every day that God will provide for us.

Jesus said, in Matthew 6, not to worry about tomorrow. Our role in raising our children is to train them to develop the habit of coming to God daily so he can meet their needs.

The habits your children are developing now are ones which they will carry with them as they grow, and which will shape who they become. Many of the habits you have now are habits your parents taught you. You shower, dress, clean your teeth, and wash your hair because of the habits you learned as a child. How much more important, then, are the spiritual disciplines and habits that help your child connect with God and receive regular strength and joy in him? They will go to these habits when they hit difficult times because you trained them well.

There's a story by R.C. Sproul that helps give us deeper understanding of the inner needs of children:

After the Korean War ended, South Korea was left with a large number of children who had been orphaned by the war. In the case of South Korea, relief agencies came in to deal with all the problems that arose in connection with having so many orphan children. One of the people involved in this relief effort told me about a problem they encountered with the children who were in the orphanages. Even though the children had three meals a day provided for them, they were restless and anxious at night and had difficulty sleeping. As they talked to the children, they soon discovered that the children had great anxiety about whether they would have food the next day. To help resolve this problem, the relief workers in one particular orphanage decided that each night when the children were put to bed, the nurses there would place a single piece of bread in each child's hand. The bread wasn't intended to be eaten; it was simply intended to be held by the children as they went to sleep. It was a "security blanket" for them, reminding them that there would be provision for their daily needs. Sure enough, the bread calmed the children's anxieties and helped them sleep. Likewise, we take comfort in knowing that our needs are met, that we have food, or "bread," for our needs.[2]

R.C. SPROUL

2 Sproul, R.C. The Prayer of the Lord. Grand Rapids: Zondervan, 2018.

Children need to know there is a God who cares.

They need to know that he is interested in the smallest detail of their lives. I've asked adults over the years if I could pray for them when they are in the middle of a difficult situation. Some, who don't really know the love of God personally, have answered, "I'm sure God has more to do than worry about my problems." This is so far from the nature of our heavenly Father. As we develop in life, we need to know our heavenly Father cares for more than just the "big" problems in the world. He cares for the smaller details, too — so much that he knows the number of hairs on our heads, and is aware of every sparrow who falls (Luke 12:6).

FOR KIDS

Think about a normal day. What do you want so that you can get through that day well?

You'll definitely need food and clothes! What else? Maybe you have a favourite toy, or there's an activity you like to do. How do those things you want help you? It's easy just to say "I want this," but if you look closely, a lot of the things we want are trying to fill a need we have. Your toy may be a good comfort when you feel alone or scared, and that's why you want it. Or playing outside could be the best place to get all of your energy out.

If you know why you want something, you can ask for the help you really need.

You can ask your parents, or other responsible grown-ups for help, and you can pray to ask Jesus for the things you need.

Talk now with your parent about the things you want today, and see if you can figure out if there is a need behind that want.

What do you really need?
What sort of things does your parent need?

God loves helping us meet our needs! We can bring them to him in prayer, and ask for him to help us. It says this in the Bible: And we are confident that he hears us whenever we ask for anything that pleases him. And since we know he hears us when we make our requests, we also know that he will give us what we ask for (1 John 5:14 –15 NLT).

Pray today for the things you and your parent need — and who else could you pray for today? It may be your family or friends, sponsor children, overseas mission partners or anyone God brings to your mind!

There is no need too great or too small for God. Do you believe that?

As your life has progressed I'm sure you have encountered deep needs that seem impossible even for God to fill, and simple needs that you haven't even taken the time to bring to God because they seem trivial. God cares about it all.

One of the great spiritual battles for parents is to keep believing in the goodness of God.

The greatest deceit of the enemy is to convince you of the lie that God doesn't care, and his blessings are not for you — but if you have surrendered your life to Christ, you live in his righteousness and the fullness of his blessing. As you teach your children to pray, "Give us this day our daily bread," make sure you pray this for yourself each day, and ask God to continually strengthen your faith to believe that he wants to answer this prayer.

Remind your children of the truth that there is no need too great or too small for God. As you pray with them, consider the needs of others so that they can know our prayers are not always about us.

GIVE US THIS DAY OUR DAILY BREAD

forgive us our sins

I want to be me.

Not many of us like talking about sin very much.

— well, not about our own. Much of the daily news is stories of people's sin, and idle talk is generally around the topic of other people's sin. So maybe we do like talking about it – but only when it belongs to someone else. Talking about our own is not as appealing.

The deepest desire of all human beings is to belong.

We want to be loved and accepted. We change who we are on the outside so the people we like will accept us, and we hide things we've done so that we won't be rejected. As we grow like this, the last thing we want is for people to know what we are really like on the inside. There is such a sense of shame that comes with revealing who we really are; our inward identity never quite matches up with our outward identity, and we desperately don't want people to know that.

When I was a secondary school teacher, I would see students doing something they weren't meant to, even things as simple as talking when they were asked to listen. But when they were called out on it, they would deny they even said a word. I had seen and heard them talking, but they would swear it wasn't them. Or they would blame someone else. They would tell their parents they were totally innocent. All this because we don't want to be wrong, in case we are not loved and accepted, and we don't want the punishment that goes with it.

Here's the amazing thing about Jesus and how he really understands the deepest needs of human beings. He understands sin and how it separates us from God and from each other — He has experienced the shame of condemnation when he hung on the cross, even though he was without sin.

He sees how we try to be better, to fit in, and yet remain alienated. And rather than condemning us for what we've done wrong, he pays the price for it. He accepts the shame, the rejection, and the accusations, and he carries it all on the cross so you don't have to be burdened by it. As you accept his pardon and he receives your sin, you receive his righteousness, and so even when you reveal your imperfections and wrongdoing to Jesus, he accepts you as you are without any condemnation or blame.

1 John 1:9 says,

"If we confess our sins, he is faithful and just to forgive us our sins and to cleanse us from all unrighteousness"

ESV

No one else can do that. That is why we try to hide from everyone else but find total acceptance and belonging with Jesus. Giving your life to Jesus means moving into a place of vulnerability before him, but instead of rejecting us he embraces us and washes away our sins.

This is where you, as the parent, play a huge role in revealing the love of God to your children. How do you respond to their sin? Some of us respond by feeling like we've failed as parents or being afraid that our children are heading on a bad trajectory.

This fear is a lack of faith that God loves you and your children enough to protect them and to give you wisdom as a parent. He loves your children. He wants them to thrive even more than you do.

He has called you to be their parent because he knows that in him you will win.

Our fear often reveals itself in the way we discipline our children, using anger, rejection, condemnation, or words of shame. Our children do need to be disciplined, but in love. Their sin is not their identity. They need to be assured that when you see who they really are, they still belong — you still love them and see the best in them. You continue to trust them, even if they let you down again. If you personally don't have this relationship with your heavenly Father, you will have trouble teaching your children to pray honestly in this way.

To learn how to confess to God and repent, your children need to see you owning up to your mistakes. If you're anything like me, you will have failed many times at home. No one in your circle of friends may have seen you say or do the wrong thing, so you hide it — but your children see and hear.

They are modelling their lives on you. They need to hear you say, "When I said that, I was wrong. That was hurtful. Would you please forgive me?" Or to hear you ask for forgiveness from your spouse, or others you might hurt. It takes humility, but the grace that comes through confession and repentance pulls people together and keeps us close to God.

Saying sorry and asking for forgiveness when you do something wrong is a big step in learning how to be responsible for your actions.

It can feel uncomfortable, because it's nice to think that we don't do anything wrong and asking forgiveness means admitting we did. But just because you want to think you did everything right, doesn't mean that's true – and it's important to face what is real and what is true, so that we can mend relationships that have been hurt, and grow from our experiences.

Admitting to God when we did something wrong gives him a chance to show us how big his love is.

Even when we've hurt him, or other people, he still loves us and accepts us. If we ask him for forgiveness, he says he *will* forgive us. People who practice this grow up to be strong, wise and kind. People who don't learn this grow older but not wiser.

What sort of things can you ask forgiveness for?

You can ask forgiveness for saying or doing something hurtful, spreading someone else's private news without their permission, lying, hitting someone or taking their things — even if you're frustrated with someone and are just wishing bad things on them.

God wants to offer you forgiveness for these things so that he can help mend any broken feelings and you can feel peaceful.

It can even be helpful to pray with someone else about the things you want to ask forgiveness for. That way they can be there to encourage you and cheer you on as you try to do better.

What is something you'd like to ask God forgiveness for today?

What is something your parent would like to ask forgiveness for today?

FOR PARENTS

Confessing sin enables us to bring into the light things that we are keeping in darkness. When we bring them to Jesus, the light of Christ can deal with them.

When we keep them to ourselves, we are trying to hide them in darkness as though the dark may obscure how wrong our sins are or how much we need someone else — Jesus — to help us deal with them.

When you are praying with your children it's good to be honest but also to be circumspect. Only share with them things they can relate to. Don't burden your children with your problems and all your failings. They are not your parents or your confidantes. Simple things, such as confessing you were angry and that was wrong, are enough to help your child see that you are real and you don't consider yourself perfect. (You may as well tell them this now as they will work it out sooner or later!)

Pray together for God's forgiveness, and know that he loves you!

You can encourage each other as you go, reminding each other that you are truly forgiven!

I, yes, I, am the One and Only,
who completely erases your sins,
never to be seen again.

I will not remember them again.
freely I do this because of who I am!

ISAIAH 43:25 TPT

as we forgive those who sin against us

I want to be like you.

Ernest Hemingway wrote a short story beginning with a Madrid joke about the very common name "Paco".

One Paco had become estranged from his father, and the father searched for him, eventually putting an ad in a Madrid newspaper with a time and place to meet, saying, "all is forgiven". When the day came, eight hundred Pacos showed up, hoping to meet their fathers for forgiveness and love.[3]

Forgiveness is a gift that only the victim can give.

True forgiveness is hard to extend because it demands that people let go of something they value — pride, a sense of justice, or maybe a desire for revenge.

You can argue for hours about who deserves to be forgiven but never really win. It all comes down to the culture of the kingdom you live in, and have chosen to embrace.

There are only two kingdoms you can choose to live in: the Kingdom of Fair or the Kingdom of Grace. Most people like the sound of fair. Your children probably have used the "fair" argument with you many times, and you have probably used it yourself, too.

3 Hemingway, Ernest. The Complete Short Stories of Ernest Hemingway. New York City: Scribner Paperback Fiction, 1987.

"Fair" simply means one person's goodness is weighed and compared with another person's goodness. When you weigh up your own and compare it with someone else's, generally you win — because most times you know your intentions more than others do, and you feel sorrier for yourself more than you do for others. In the Kingdom of Fair, everyone gets what they deserve according to their own worthiness. And that's fine until you start to get what you actually deserve.

In the Kingdom of Grace, everyone gets what they don't deserve. They are forgiven, even when they don't deserve it.

They are blessed when they don't earn it. They are loved when they are unlovely and accepted when they have been rejected.

Choose which kingdom you like. Whether you are aware of it or not, you make this choice every day.

Having tried both, I prefer the Kingdom of Grace, where I get what I don't deserve. As a result of this broken world, I still get things I wish that I didn't — my family and I have received many things we don't want and don't deserve more than anyone else, including the loss of one of our children. But in the Kingdom of Grace we also receive wonderful gifts that we don't deserve — the kindness and grace of God, who heals, restores, and gives life, and hope, and goodness. The Kingdom of Fair still suffers the injustices of this broken world, but it cannot offer me the healing of the Kingdom of Grace.

When my children had a hard time with friends, I would listen to their pain and sorrow, and comfort them if they were crying, but also lead them to forgive.

As one who was bullied at school, I discovered that resentment towards those friends carried into adulthood, and affected the way I saw myself. It had a power over me that I was largely unaware of. It was only when I moved into the Kingdom of Grace and forgave those friends that my sense of identity changed as well. Nothing had changed to make those friends deserve my forgiveness, but by operating in the Kingdom of Grace, I was able not only to receive what was undeserved, but also to give it.

Teaching your children to forgive is a wonderful gift that sets them free to be the person God created them to be.

They are no longer slaves to the hurts and opinions of others. They become like Jesus, learning to love and bless those around them rather than only ever reacting to what has been done to them. This is one of the great ways that your children can bring God's kingdom into the world. Forgiveness offered through the cross of Christ sets us free from the spiritual powers of this world, and ushers us into his kingdom, which operates in a totally different and liberating way.

Forgiving doesn't mean that what happened doesn't matter.

It actually requires for you to acknowledge the pain, and then to say, "I release you from the debt of what you have taken from me because Jesus graciously restores to me everything that I have lost." I've discovered that helping my children to forgive frees them from carrying a lot of unnecessary pain into their future, and enables them to move forward in confidence of their value. I've also discovered that forgiveness is a lifestyle and a habit. Every day I need to forgive, often more than once.

I still struggle with it at times when it seems unfair — there's something in me that often wants to run back to the Kingdom of Fair — but God in his mercy keeps reminding me of his grace, and the price he paid for my forgiveness, and so I turn back to his kingdom, reminding myself it's the only place I want to be.

FOR KIDS

When you hurt someone, you're meant to ask for forgiveness.

It can be really hard to admit you're in the wrong. But what about when someone hurts *you* and now you need to forgive them? Maybe they've apologized and asked for forgiveness, or maybe they haven't. You might feel angry at them for what they did, or scared of them. You might not want to forgive them, ever.

Forgiving someone doesn't mean saying that what they did is okay.

It hurt you, a little bit or a lot, and it was definitely wrong of them to do that. If saying you forgive them doesn't change the wrong they did, what does it do?

Holding on to your hurt feelings encourages you to keep on feeling that way. Those feelings end up controlling how you see yourself and others, because they stand between you and the situation, blocking your view of God's goodness with the pain you experienced.

Forgiving someone who has hurt you can be as easy as saying that you forgive them, and letting go of those hurt feelings straight away, or if they've hurt you in a big way, it might mean forgiving them over and over in your heart, as many times as it takes for you to stop seeing the hurt they gave you as bigger than God's goodness.

God has such a wonderful future planned especially for you. He knows that you are important, and he loves you so much.

God doesn't want you to live looking at the ways people have hurt you — he wants you to live in excitement of his plans for your life!

You get to forgive other people and live in freedom and grace, and in turn God forgives you, putting aside everything you have done that could hurt him so that he can see the very best in you.

If you're not ready to forgive someone, you can pray for God to give you the strength and love to forgive.

You may like to use a simple prayer like this:

Father, I am having a hard time forgiving _____ for _____. Please give me your love in my heart so I can forgive them just like you have forgiven me. Amen.

After that, pray this prayer to forgive them:

Father, I forgive _____ for_____. May you bless them, and may they know you more each day. Amen.

You can pray this as many times as you need to.

God is on your side, and he wants you living free of the hurt people have caused, not because the hurt doesn't matter, but because you matter so much more than it does.

FOR PARENTS

Do not let the sun go down while you are still angry, and do not give the devil a foothold.

EPHESIANS 4:26 NIV

Unforgiveness becomes a foothold for the enemy to invade your life. Because of the undeserved grace of God, we live with every spiritual blessing from the heavenly realms. We stand with Jesus, our advocate, who declares us righteous in him. When we choose to **point the accusing finger at others, we live by the devil's** example, who spends his time accusing others (Rev 12:10), and by taking his example we choose to live on his side, instead of in the fullness of God's blessing.

Forgiveness is more than a nice thing to do.

It holds great spiritual and emotional power.

The simple principle of not letting the sun go down on our anger is a reminder to make a habit that before the day is over, we allow the Holy Spirit to search our hearts, and show us anything that would be a barrier between us and the abundant life in Christ. As you make this a daily habit, you will experience the freedom and blessing of living in forgiveness, and you will find it easy to teach your child to forgive. And remember Jesus' words:

"For if you forgive other people when they sin against you, your heavenly Father will also forgive you. But if you do not forgive others their sins, your Father will not forgive your sins."

MATTHEW 6:14-15 NIV

This is not because God is punishing you but because, with unforgiveness in your heart, you are walking out of the realm of grace, and into the realm of judgment — that Kingdom of Fair.

Let God do the judging.
Let us enjoy his freedom.

lead us
not into
temptation
but deliver
us from evil

I want to flourish.

I love to speak blessing and hope into my children. My parents spoke blessing and hope into me, with compassion for where I was, and anticipation for the life I had ahead, and it led me to want to be the person they saw — someone better than who I saw in myself.

This part of the Lord's Prayer, "Lead us not into temptation but deliver us from evil," is not so much about what not to do but about who we are created to be. The truth is that all of us have fallen short of the glory of God, but that's not where we are meant to stay. We are meant to become the glorious and free children of God, who rise against temptation and evil, and live lives of dignity that reveal the beauty and power of God.

Your children need to have their identity prophesied over them.

When my children gave in to temptation, as we all do, I would make sure I reminded them that what they did is not who they are. I reminded them that they were an amazing and wonderful boy or girl, and a specially chosen child of God. I spoke to them of their true identity and of the unique qualities I saw in them — and still do.

"When someone prophesies, he speaks to encourage people, to build them up, and to bring them comfort."

1 CORINTHIANS 14:3 TPT

As a parent ministering to your children, make words of encouragement, strengthening and comfort a habit in prayer. Prophecy is a form of prayer you can use daily.

God has chosen you and your children to experience abundant life and blessing. Look at this passage, and as you read it, remind yourself that there is an enemy waiting to lure you away from all of this goodness that God has for you. That temptation can lead you to a life where you miss out on the fullness of life that God, in his grace, wants to give you.

If you fully obey the Lord your God and carefully follow all his commands I give you today, the Lord your God will set you high above all the nations on earth. All these blessings will come on you and accompany you if you obey the Lord your God:

You will be blessed in the city and blessed in the country.

The fruit of your womb will be blessed, and the crops of your land and the young of your livestock—the calves of your herds and the lambs of your flocks.

Your basket and your kneading trough will be blessed.

You will be blessed when you come in and blessed when you go out.

The Lord will grant that the enemies who rise up against you will be defeated before you. They will come at you from one direction but flee from you in seven.

The Lord will send a blessing on your barns and on everything you put your hand to. The Lord your God will bless you in the land he is giving you.

The Lord will establish you as his holy people, as he promised you on oath, if you keep the commands of the Lord your God and walk in obedience to him. Then all the peoples on earth will see that you are called by the name of the Lord, and they will fear you. The Lord will grant you abundant prosperity—in the fruit of your womb, the young of your livestock and the crops of your ground—in the land he swore to your ancestors to give you.

The Lord will open the heavens, the storehouse of his bounty, to send rain on your land in season and to bless all the work of your hands. You will lend to many nations but will borrow from none. The Lord will make you the head, not the tail. If you pay attention to the commands of the Lord your God that I give you this day and carefully follow them, you will always be at the top, never at the bottom. Do not turn aside from any of the commands I give you today, to the right or to the left, following other gods and serving them.

DEUTERONOMY 28:1-14 NIV

Jesus asks us to pray, "lead us not into temptation but deliver us from evil" because he doesn't want us to live subject to evil. He wants us to live in his blessing. You don't want to be subject to evil and you don't want that for your children.

As you see yourself as a parent empowered by the Spirit of God, you will have great hope for your family not because of what you deserve but because of his grace.

God has an amazing vision for our life ahead, but it seems like we mess up his plans when we sin, or do something wrong. Yet even when we mess it up — our sin shows us that we aren't perfect, and so we really need him and his grace, and he can still work it together for good.

God forgives us a lot, and he'll keep on forgiving us as long as we keep asking him for it.

There are two ways here that we get to show people his goodness: by accepting that we have done the wrong thing and receiving God's grace, and by asking him to help us not to do the wrong thing in the first place.

God loves you so much. He has made you his child and thinks you can be the sort of person to help him spread his kingdom of love.

He doesn't see you as someone who keeps on messing up and needs to get better at doing the right thing — he sees you as someone who is learning how to do the right thing. That means sometimes you need to ask for help so you can understand what is right and what is wrong, or even just so you can want to do what is right when the wrong thing seems more fun. And God would love to help you!

FOR KIDS

So remember who God says you really are, and when you need help, ask him for it!

I am the wonderful creation of a loving God. He knows everything about me.

PSALM 139:13-14

I was made to reflect the image of God. My abilities to create, learn, and love come from him. I have so much in common with the Creator.

GENESIS 1:27

I am adopted into God's family, and I will live for eternity as his child.

ROMANS 8:15

I've been created with a purpose. God has prepared good works for me to do, and he will give me everything I need to carry them out.

EPHESIANS 2:10

I was chosen by God, and I am special to him.

1 PETER 2:9

I am a citizen of heaven; this world is not my home.

PHILIPPIANS 3:20

Temptation itself isn't a sin — remember Jesus was tempted, but never sinnec.

Temptation is the point at which we choose the next path to take.

The fact that we are tempted reminds us that we have free will.

Dealing with temptation is how we become strong individuals who have learnz. by the power of the Holy Spirit, to live above what feels good at the moment, and to choose to follow the Spirit of God.

As we do, we are transformed into the dignified and glorious human beings we were created to be. We reflect the image of God.

In the end, that's who we al want to be.

Teaching your children to pray, "Lead us not into temptation," is more about seeing who they are becoming, rather than what they shouldn't do.

When we have a vision of who we were created to be, temptation becomes far easier to overcome.

Each of us has particular areas where we are more prone to temptation. What are yours?

Whatever it may be, it all has a common root — we are tempted with something that we believe will satisfy us more than Jesus. Giving in to this temptation destroys our value, our dignity, and our beauty as God's creation.

As you, as the parent, have a vision for who you are becoming, you will be better able to lead your children in the same way.

for yours is the kingdom, the power, and the glory, now and forever

I want everyone to see how wonderful you are.

Scholars generally believe this conclusion to the Lord's prayer was not in the original manuscripts. It takes the form of a doxology — a short hymn-like verse which exalts the glory of God at the end of a psalm or prayer. An example of a doxology similar to this line of the Lord's Prayer is found in King David's prayer located in 1 Chronicles 29:11–13 of the Old Testament (NIV).

Yours, Lord, is the greatness and the power
and the glory and the majesty and the splendour,
for everything in heaven and earth is yours.

Yours, Lord, is the kingdom;
you are exalted as head over all.

Wealth and honor come from you;
you are the ruler of all things.

In your hands are strength and power
to exalt and give strength to all.

Now, our God, we give you thanks,
and praise your glorious name.

In the early Church, the Christians living in the eastern half of the Roman Empire added this doxology to the Gospel text when praying together.

Do you notice how this doxology begins with "for?" How good it is to remind ourselves why we pray as Jesus taught us to pray! We often live under the illusion that we are in control of our lives.

The truth is that whether we surrender our lives to him or not, ultimately the kingdom, the power, and the glory are his.

Even with free will, it only takes us a day at the beach and a powerful wave to remind ourselves of the little control we have in life when we try to design our own little kingdoms.

He gives us the keys to his kingdom, he fills us with his power and invites us to share in his glory.

Teaching this to our children is paramount in understanding our relationship with God and prayer. It is vital in the development of children so that they will become wellrounded, God-focused and others-focused human beings who make a difference in the world for good.

The Lord's Prayer is not just a prayer we are to memorize and recite back to God — it is only an example of how we pray as Jesus taught us to pray. Does this mean it is wrong to memorize the Lord's Prayer? Of course not! There's nothing wrong with simply praying the Lord's Prayer from memory, if your heart is in it and you truly mean the words you say.

Remember, in prayer, God is far more interested in our communicating with him and speaking from our hearts than he is in the specific words we use.

When I was child, I learned the Lord's Prayer by heart. As I grew, I learned to take the prayer and make it my own, praying each line my own way. It has helped me grow in a deep and beautiful relationship with my heavenly Father that is personal and everlasting. We have had our ups and downs in relationship through the good and bad times of life — I have questioned him and doubted his love; but more than that I have learned to rejoice in him and experience in greater fullness his joy, hope and love.

I know that without him, I wouldn't be where I am today, but one of the reasons our relationship is secure is because I had parents who took the time to teach me to pray, and gave me a framework for prayer that I could take with me wherever I go. I know that his is the kingdom, and the power, and the glory — and that gives me every reason to rely on him always and to talk to him as each day unfolds, trusting in his unfailing love.

FOR KIDS

What is the greatest power you can imagine? Or consider your favourite superhero. Whatever power or superhero you can imagine, God is far greater than all of them. In fact there is no other power that is greater than God.

When you pray, "For yours is the kingdom, and the power, and the glory," you are joining his team – the team that always wins.

You are saying to God that you belong to him. You are giving your life to him and trusting him with everything. You choose to obey him in everything because you know he has ultimate power, and he always wins every battle for those on his team. The good news about this, is that you don't earn it by being good. You simply say "yes" to him every day in every way. When you pray, "For yours is the kingdom, and the power, and the glory," pray it with joy and excitement. This is great news!

This is a great prayer for a parent. Often you feel the weight of responsibility. You want the best for your children, and love them so much, but you are also aware of your imperfections and failures. It's so important to remind yourself that your loving heavenly Father is omnipotent, omniscient, and omnipresent.

As you trust yourself and your children into his protection and his plans, you will see him triumph over everything.

Spend time simply declaring this over yourself and your family every day in confidence that nothing can ever separate you from the love of God.

No, in all these things we are more than conquerors through him who loved us. For I am convinced that neither death nor life, neither angels nor demons, neither the present nor the future, nor any powers, neither height nor depth, nor anything else in all creation, will be able to separate us from the love of God that is in Christ Jesus our Lord.

ROMANS 8:37-39 NIV

FINISHING TOGETHER

Jesus taught his disciples a simple prayer to help us all understand how to really engage with God in prayer.

He wants us to remember God's holiness, and the mission he gives us to bring the kingdom of Heaven here to earth. He wants us to remember that God gives us what we need to live well every day, and that he forgives us for everything because he took the punishment for our sins. He asks us to forgive others in the same generous manner. He wants us to call on God when we need help to do the right thing in order to become the amazing people we were created to be.

And finally, Jesus wants to remind us that God really is the one in charge of everything — he is the king who is in control, he is love and he deserves our praise!

Even though The Lord's Prayer is deep and powerful, it is still very short, which is why so many people can engage with it.

Read it today, tomorrow, and as often as you need to.

Use it as the basis for your prayer throughout the day, and memorize it so that you can pray as Jesus taught us to pray:

Our Father in heaven,
hallowed be your name,
your kingdom come,
your will be done,
on earth as it is in heaven.
Give us today our daily bread.
And forgive us our debts,
as we also have forgiven our debtors.
And lead us not into temptation,
but deliver us from the evil one.
For yours is the kingdom and the power and glory forever.
Amen.

MATTHEW 6:9-13 NIV

BIBLIOGRAPHY

Hemingway, Ernest. *The Complete Short Stories of Ernest Hemingway.* New York City: Scribner Paperback Fiction, 1987.

Hunt, Gladys. *Honey for a Child's Heart: The Imaginative Use of Books in Family Life, Fourth Edition.* Grand Rapids: Zondervan, 2002.

Sproul, R.C. *The Prayer of the Lord.* Grand Rapids: Zondervan, 2018.